MUGGIE MA[GGIE]

MW01278424

by
Beverly Cleary

Student Packet

Written by
Sammie Underwood

Contains masters for:

1 Prereading Activity
4 Vocabulary Activities
1 Study Guide
2 Creative Writing Activities
2 Character Analysis Activities
1 Critical Thinking Activity
1 Comprehension Activity
2 Literary Analysis Activities
1 Art Activity
2 Quizzes
1 Novel Test

PLUS Detailed Answer Key
and Scoring Rubric

Note

The 1991 Avon Books, Inc. paperback edition of the book, © 1990 by Beverly Cleary, was used to prepare this guide. Page references may differ in other editions. Novel ISBN: 0-380-71087-0

Please note: Please assess the appropriateness of this novel for the age level and maturity of your students prior to reading and discussing it with them.

ISBN-10: 1-58130-532-X
ISBN-13: 978-1-58130-532-6

Andrea M. Harris, Production Manager/Production Specialist
Michael Hanna, Product Development Specialist
A. Taylor Henderson, Product Development Specialist
Heather M. Marnan, Product Development Specialist
Suzanne K. Mammen, Curriculum Specialist
Gabriela Mongiello, Product Development Specialist
Jill Reed, Product Development Specialist
Adrienne Speer, Production Specialist

Be a Detective!

Directions: Check out the book by looking at the cover and thumbing through the pages. Then, ask yourself who, what, where, when, why, and how. Write your questions in the spaces below. Exchange papers with a partner and answer each other's questions.

Who?
_____
_____
_____
_____

When?
_____
_____
_____
_____

What?
_____
_____
_____
_____

Why?
_____
_____
_____
_____
_____

Where?
_____
_____
_____
_____

How?
_____
_____
_____
_____

Vocabulary Chart

cootie (1)	cockapoo (2)	monitor (3)	forecast (3)
cursive (7)	contrary (8)	nuisance (11)	indignant (11)
salute (13)	graceful (14)	roller coaster (14)	examined (18)
artistic (18)			

Directions: Write each vocabulary word in the left-hand column of the chart. Complete the chart by placing a check mark in the column that best describes your familiarity with each word. Working with a partner, find and read the line where each word appears in the story. Find the meaning of each word in the dictionary. Together with your partner, choose ten of the words checked in the last column. On a separate sheet of paper, use each of those words in a sentence.

Vocabulary Word	I Can Define	I Have Seen/Heard	New Word For Me

Name _____

experimented (21)	veterinarian (22)	reluctant (24)	immature (24)
dawdled (25)	motivated (27)	psychologist (28)	suspicious (29)
revolt (30)	individual (31)	signatures (32)	daintily (32)
citizens (36)			

Directions: Solve the following crossword puzzle.

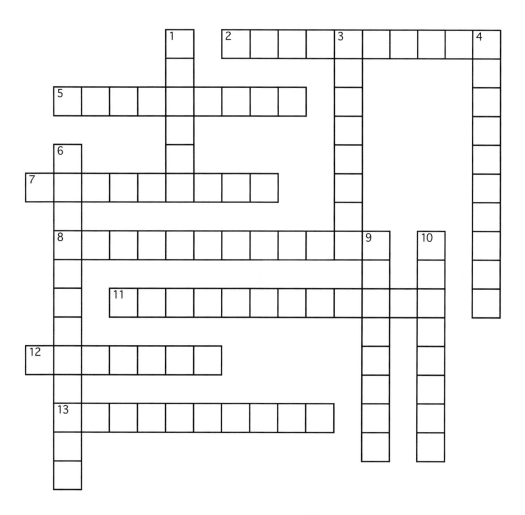

Across

2 wary
5 inspired
7 unwilling
8 tested
11 doctor of the mind and behavior
12 delayed
13 separate

Down

1 mutiny
3 young
4 autographs
6 animal doctor
9 prettily
10 inhabitants of a city, state, etc.

Name _____

briefcase (40)	virtuous (40)	consonant (40)	ashamed (41)
accurate (43)	whispering (44)	scrunched (44)	invisible (44)
escaping (47)	supervised (47)	replaced (51)	

Directions: Write each word in the correct column. Then write two sentences that include one word from each column.

Adjectives	Nouns	Verbs

1. _____

_____

2. _____

_____

© Novel Units, Inc.

shabby (52)	snatched (52)	peculiar (53)	ferocious (55)
tittered (55)	frantically (57)	privacy (59)	distinguished (61)
reform (61)	arithmetic (63)	crumple (64)	remains (64)
crisis (66)	congratulations (66)	astonished (66)	

Directions: Circle the correct answer.

1. The shirt was shabby. Was the shirt new or worn out?

2. The lion was ferocious. Was the lion gentle or wild?

3. I found the remains of my baby blanket stored in the attic. Was it new or used?

4. My dog has reformed. Has my dog stayed the same or improved?

5. That looks peculiar. Does it look normal or weird?

6. The first-grade class tittered. Did they giggle or cry?

7. Sue wants her privacy. Does she want company or time alone?

8. My papers are all crumpled. Are they crunched or smooth?

9. Joe snatched the cookie. Did he release it or grab it?

10. Mom looked frantically for the keys. Did she look for the keys excitedly or calmly?

11. Dad looks distinguished. Does he look tacky or elegant?

12. I like arithmetic. Do I like experiments or calculations?

13. The teacher is astonished. Is she surprised or unmoved?

14. I have one crisis after another. Do I have good luck or misfortune?

15. My teacher said, "Congratulations!" Did she mean better luck next time or well done?

Directions: Answer the following questions on a separate sheet of paper. Use the questions to guide your reading and prepare for class discussion.

Chapter 1, pp. 1–12

1. What do the fourth-grade boys tell Maggie about third grade?

2. Who sits at Maggie's table at school?

3. What nickname does Maggie's mom call her? What nickname does her father call her?

4. Who is Ms. Madden?

5. Give three reasons why Maggie does not want to write cursive.

Chapter 2, pp. 13–20

1. To what does Mrs. Leeper compare cursive letters?

2. Why can't Maggie stay after school to talk to Mrs. Leeper?

3. Describe Mrs. Schultz's cursive.

4. Describe Mr. Schultz's cursive.

Chapter 3, pp. 21–29

1. What word does Mrs. Leeper use to describe Maggie's cursive?

2. Why does Mrs. Leeper think Maggie is not writing cursive?

3. What kind of student does Maggie think she is?

4. Why does Mr. Galloway think Maggie is not writing cursive?

Chapter 4, pp. 30–36

1. Why does Jo Ann, Maggie's friend, think Maggie refuses to write cursive?

2. How does Maggie decide to compromise?

3. How does Maggie get the name "Muggie Maggie"?

Chapter 5, pp. 37–43

1. What present does Ms. Madden send Maggie?

2. Describe Maggie's thank-you note to Ms. Madden.

3. What is Ms. Madden's response?

4. How does Maggie feel about Ms. Madden's response?

5. What does Maggie want to be when she grows up?

Chapter 6, pp. 44–51

1. What is funny about the words Mrs. Leeper writes on the chalkboard?

2. What do the words cause Maggie to discover?

3. Why does Maggie think she will not be chosen as message monitor?

4. What does Maggie recognize in Mrs. Leeper's note to Mr. Galloway?

5. What word jumps out at Maggie from Mr. Galloway's note to Mrs. Leeper?

6. Why is cursive suddenly very interesting to Maggie?

Chapter 7, pp. 52–61

1. What does Maggie discover about the notes she delivers?

2. What does Maggie do all weekend?

3. By Sunday, how well can Maggie read cursive?

4. What does Maggie tell her parents about their cursive?

5. How does Maggie feel after the long weekend?

Chapter 8, pp. 62–70

1. How does Mrs. Leeper know that Maggie can read cursive?

2. How does Mr. Galloway know that Maggie can read cursive?

3. What does Maggie expect Mrs. Leeper to say when she goes back to class?

4. What does Mrs. Leeper actually do and say?

5. What compliment does Maggie give Mrs. Leeper?

6. What decision does Maggie make?

7. What does Kirby call Maggie?

8. How does Maggie respond to Kirby?

Name _____

Directions: Write a newspaper article about a pet that needs a home.

Pick-a-Pet

Wednesday, October 2 • Section A, Page 1

Name _____

Directions: The phrases in the left column describe a gifted and talented person. In the right column, write examples of Maggie's attitudes or behaviors that demonstrate the traits listed.

Gifted and Talented Traits	Maggie's Behaviors
1. Desire to learn	
2. Intense or unusual interests	
3. Expressive with words	
4. Exceptional memory	
5. Questions and explores	
6. Quickly grasps new concepts and connections	
7. Has many original ideas	
8. Strong reactions	
9. Pursues self-selected tasks	

Directions: Look at a cursive alphabet. Write each uppercase letter in the column where it belongs. When you are finished, continue with the lowercase letters.

No Loops	One Loop	Two or More Loops

The following is a poem about math problems.

It's better to eat worms
with ketchup and cream
or to be the last pick
or have a skinned knee
than work the hard problems
on page one hundred and three.

Directions: Write a similar poem about cursive by finishing the lines below. Look at the example above for ideas.

Line 1: It's better to _____

Line 2: with _____

Line 3: or _____

Line 4: or _____

Line 5: than _____

Line 6: _____ (write something about line 5 that
rhymes with line 4)

After you have finished your poem, copy it onto another sheet of paper and illustrate it.

Name _____

Directions: Read the following sentences. Mark them with an "F" for fact or an "O" for opinion.

_____ 1. Mrs. Schultz teaches exercise classes five mornings a week.

_____ 2. Mrs. Leeper is the nicest teacher.

_____ 3. Kisser needs exercise.

_____ 4. We start cursive next week.

_____ 5. Cursive is hard.

_____ 6. You'll enjoy cursive once you start.

_____ 7. Kisser is lucky because he doesn't have to write cursive.

_____ 8. Today is a happy day.

_____ 9. You're supposed to close loops on letters to have neat handwriting.

_____ 10. Maggie is too immature to write cursive.

_____ 11. The school psychologist is a nice person.

12. Write two facts and two opinions about cursive.

13. Write two facts and two opinions about pets.

14. Write two facts and two opinions about Maggie.

Character Web

Directions: Complete the attribute web below by filling in information about Maggie.

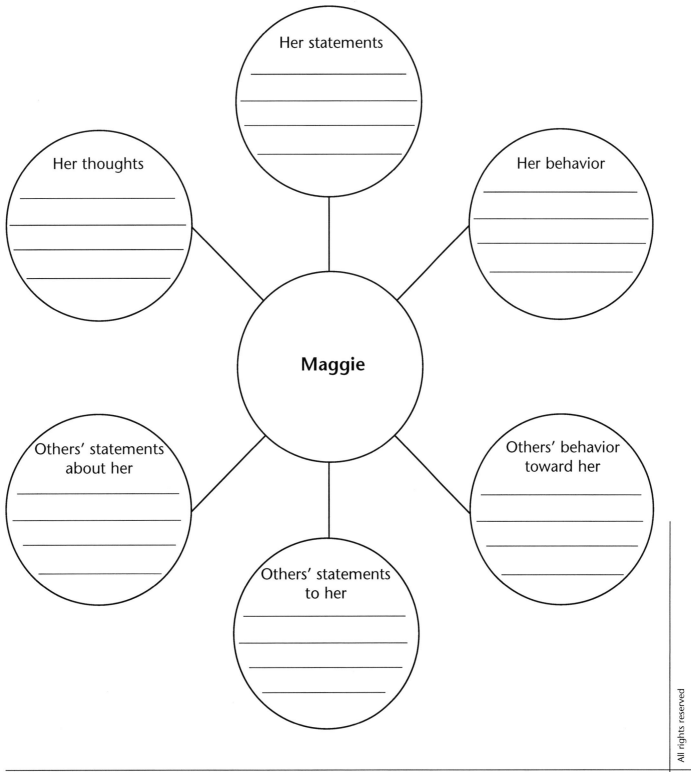

Name _____

Directions: Draw your favorite scene from the novel. Then, explain your drawing and why you chose that scene.

```


```

_____

_____

_____

_____

_____

_____

_____

Name _____

Idioms are words, phrases, or expressions that cannot be taken literally. Mrs. Leeper said that she had eyes in the back of her head. Do you think she really did?

Directions: Read the following idioms. Write what they really mean. Draw a picture that illustrates the literal meaning of the idiom.

1. I was caught red-handed taking the candy.

3. That test was a piece of cake. I am sure I got all the answers right.

2. Mary and Sue can't do cartwheels in P.E. class. They are in the same boat.

4. Yesterday we had a huge storm. It was raining cats and dogs.

Name _____

Story Map

Directions: Complete the story map.

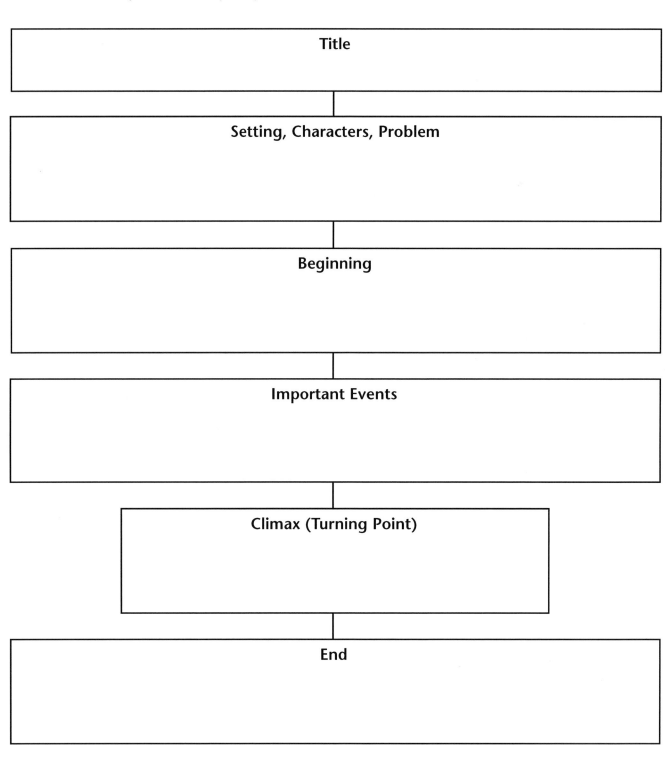

Title

Setting, Characters, Problem

Beginning

Important Events

Climax (Turning Point)

End

Name _____

A. Fill in the Blanks

1. The fourth-grade boys insist that third grade is _____, cursive writing is _____, and Mrs. Leeper is _____.

2. Maggie's mom calls her _____, and her dad calls her _____.

3. Mrs. Leeper compares some cursive letters to a _____ _____.

4. Maggie thinks of herself as a _____ and _____ student.

5. Maggie doesn't close the letter _____ in her name, so it looks like the letter _____. This makes her name _____ instead of Maggie.

6. Mrs. Leeper sends Maggie to see the _____ and the _____ _____ because she will not write cursive.

7. Mr. Schultz motivates Maggie by not allowing her to use the _____.

8. Maggie decides she will not be giving in if she just writes her _____ in cursive.

B. Short Answer: Explain why Maggie doesn't want to write cursive. Write your answer on the lines below.

_____

_____

_____

_____

_____

_____

Name _____

A. True/False

____ 1. Ms. Madden sends Maggie a set of colored pencils.

____ 2. Ms. Madden likes Maggie's thank-you note.

____ 3. Maggie is chosen to be the message monitor.

____ 4. Maggie recognizes her name in Mr. Galloway's letter to Mrs. Leeper.

____ 5. Maggie becomes interested in cursive when she realizes that she can't read other people's letters.

____ 6. Maggie studies cursive in her room for two hours.

____ 7. Maggie teaches herself to read cursive.

____ 8. Mr. Galloway never discovers that Maggie can read cursive.

____ 9. Mr. Galloway's cursive is the neatest of all.

____ 10. Maggie decides that she will write cursive forever.

B. Short Answer: Describe how Maggie teaches herself to read and write cursive. Write your answer on the lines below.

_____

_____

_____

_____

_____

_____

_____

_____

Name _____

A. Matching: Match each quote with the character who said it.

_____ 1. Mrs. Schultz

_____ 2. Mr. Schultz

_____ 3. Jo Ann

_____ 4. Kirby

_____ 5. Ms. Madden

_____ 6. Mrs. Leeper

_____ 7. Mr. Galloway

_____ 8. Maggie

a. "Hello there, Maggie. Sit down and let's have a little talk."

b. "I'm left-handed, and my teachers didn't show me how to turn my paper."

c. "…why didn't you copy your letter over?"

d. "How many of you have ridden on a roller coaster?"

e. "Kisser is not a nuisance. Kisser is a loving dog."

f. "No more computer for you. You stay strictly away from it."

g. "How come you're delivering so many messages?"

h. "If you are having trouble, maybe I can help you on Saturday."

B. Multiple Choice: Choose the BEST answer to each question.

_____ 9. Which of the following is NOT a reason why Maggie refuses to write cursive?
  A Books are not written in cursive.
  B She can print or use the computer.
  C It's all wrinkled and stuck together.
  D She is too immature to write cursive.

_____ 10. What kind of student is Maggie?
  A average
  B slow learner
  C gifted and talented
  D rude and disruptive

_____ 11. How does Maggie compromise?
  A by writing cursive with her left hand
  B by writing cursive on important papers
  C by trying her best to learn to write cursive
  D by writing cursive like a grown-up, just for her signature

____ 12. How does Maggie get the nickname "Muggie Maggie"?
    A She doesn't know her letters.
    B Her dad calls her angry face a "mug."
    C Mrs. Leeper calls her this one day by accident and it sticks.
    D She doesn't close the "a" in her name, so it looks like a "u."

____ 13. Why does Mrs. Leeper choose Maggie as the message monitor?
    A Maggie is the teacher's pet.
    B Maggie is gifted and talented and can do a good job.
    C Maggie cannot read the notes because she cannot read cursive.
    D She hopes Maggie will be interested in reading the notes and will learn cursive.

____ 14. What word(s) jumps out at Maggie from Mr. Galloway's note to Mrs. Leeper?
    A the date
    B thank you
    C Maggie's name
    D Mrs. Leeper's name

C. Short Answer: Write a brief answer for each of the following questions.

15. Describe why Maggie decides not to write cursive.

16. Describe the results of Maggie's decision at home and at school.

17. List at least five examples from the novel that show Maggie is gifted and talented.

18. Do you think Mrs. Leeper's method to motivate Maggie to write cursive was successful? Describe another method she could have tried and tell what you think the result might have been.

Answer Key

Activity #1: Questions will vary.

Activity #2: Answers will vary.

Activity #3:

(Crossword puzzle solution)
Across: SUSPICIOUS, MOTIVATED, RELUCTANT, EXPERIMENTED, PSYCHOLOGIST, DAWDLED, INDIVIDUAL

Activity #4: Adjectives: accurate, ashamed, virtuous, invisible; Nouns: briefcase, consonant; Verbs: whispering, escaping, scrunched, supervised, replaced

Activity #5: 1. worn out 2. wild 3. used 4. improved 5. weird 6. giggle 7. time alone 8. crunched 9. grab it 10. excitedly 11. elegant 12. calculations 13. surprised 14. misfortune 15. well done

Study Guide

Chapter 1, pp. 1–12: 1. They say that third grade is awful, cursive writing is hard, and Mrs. Leeper is mean (p. 2). 2. Courtney, Kelly, and Kirby Jones (p. 3) 3. Angelface; Goldilocks (pp. 2–4) 4. Maggie's father's secretary who often sends her presents (p. 6) 5. It's all wrinkled and stuck together. She can use the computer. Books are not written in cursive (pp. 8–12).

Chapter 2, pp. 13–20: 1. Mrs. Leeper compares them to roller coasters (p. 14). 2. She has to catch the bus (p. 18). 3. Her cursive leans over backward and has little circles for the dots over the "i" (p. 18). 4. He doesn't close loops on letters that hang down (p. 20).

Chapter 3, pp. 21–29: 1. untidy (p. 21) 2. She is too immature (p. 24). 3. gifted and talented (p. 24) 4. She's not motivated (p. 27).

Chapter 4, pp. 30–36: 1. She thinks Maggie is having trouble (p. 31). 2. by writing just her signature like a grown-up (p. 32) 3. Maggie doesn't close the "a" in her name, which makes it look like a "u" (p. 36).

Chapter 5, pp. 37–43: 1. a ballpoint pen that writes in blue and red (p. 37) 2. She writes one letter in red and one letter in blue throughout the letter. Then she writes a note using one big letter "S" to write "Sorry So Sloppy" (pp. 39–40). 3. She asks Maggie why she did not copy her letter over (p. 41). 4. She is ashamed (p. 41). 5. astronaut or meter maid (p. 43)

Chapter 6, pp. 44–51: 1. She writes "mouth of September mice day" instead of "month of September nice day" (p. 46). 2. She cannot read cursive (p. 46). 3. She does not make Mrs. Leeper happy (p. 46). 4. a question mark (p. 48) 5. Maggie's name (p. 49–50) 6. She wants to read the letters (p. 51).

Chapter 7, pp. 52–61: 1. She can puzzle them out with enough time (p. 56). 2. study cursive (p. 59) 3. She can read cursive as long as it is neat (p. 59). 4. how to improve it (pp. 60–61) 5. tired and cross (p. 61)

Chapter 8, pp. 62–70: 1. She sees Maggie read the note written in cursive on the chalkboard (p. 63). 2. He notices the way she acts when she brings the note to his office (p. 66). 3. something about cursive (p. 67) 4. gives her a hug and says, "This is a happy day, Maggie" (p. 67) 5. that her cursive is the neatest of all the teachers (p. 69) 6. She will write cursive for now and decide later how to write when she is a grown-up (p. 69). 7. Muggie Maggie and teacher's pet (p. 69) 8. She writes him a note in cursive (pp. 69–70).

Note: Answers to Activities #6–14 will vary. Suggested answers are given where applicable.

Activity #6: Suggestions: Include a description—size, color, qualities, special abilities, etc.

Activity #7: Suggested Answers: 1. She reads chapter books (p. 12). 2. She wants to be an astronaut or a meter maid (p. 43). 3. "Kisser is not a nuisance. Kisser is a loving dog" (p. 11). 4. She remembers the details about cursive that Mrs. Leeper tells the class (pp. 18–19). 5. She questions why all of Mrs. Leeper's notes look the same (p. 53). 6. She studies cursive on her own (p. 57). 7. She writes fancy letters to Ms. Madden (p. 39). 8. Her eyes fill with tears when she reads Ms. Madden's letter (p. 41). 9. She spends the weekend in her room practicing cursive (p. 57).

Activity #8: Suggestions: uppercase no loops: A, I, P; one loop: B, C, F, G, K, M, N, O, R, S, T, U, V, W; two or more loops: D, E, H, J, L, Q, X, Y, Z; lowercase no loops: a, c, d, i, m, n, o, r, s, t, u, v, w, y; one loop: b, e, g, h, j, k, l, p, q, y, z; two or more loops: f

Activity #9: Suggestion:

It's better to kiss frogs

with green slimy skin

or pull a loose tooth

or rake leaves in the fall

than learn cursive letters

both capital and small.

Activity #10: 1. F 2. O 3. F 4. F 5. O 6. O 7. O 8. O 9. F 10. O 11. O 12.–14. Answers will vary.

Activity #11: Suggestions: Her statements—"I'm not going to write cursive" (p. 9). Her behavior—contrary (p. 9); Others' behavior toward her—teacher thinks she's immature (p. 24); Others' statements to her—"teacher's pet" (p. 69); Others' statements about her—Maggie is a "bright kid" (p. 56). Her thoughts—"Cursive is dumb" (p. 8).

Activity #12: Answers will vary.

Activity #13: Answers will vary.

Activity #14: Title—*Muggie Maggie*; Setting, Characters, Problem—Maggie's home and school; Maggie, Mrs. Schultz, Mr. Schultz, Mrs. Leeper, Jo Ann, Courtney, Kirby, Ms. Madden, Kisser; Maggie doesn't want to learn to write cursive. Beginning—It is Maggie's first day in third grade. She rides the bus home and announces to her parents that her class will learn cursive soon. Important Events— Maggie visits the principal's office, Maggie becomes message monitor, Maggie spends a weekend in her room trying to learn cursive, Maggie recognizes her name in one of the notes. Climax (Turning Point)—Maggie is desperate to read the notes teachers send each other, so she decides to learn to read and write cursive. End—Maggie learns to write cursive. She decides she will write cursive for now and later decide how she will write when she is grown-up.

Quiz #1: A. 1. awful, hard, mean (p. 2) 2. Angelface, Goldilocks (pp. 2–4) 3. roller coaster (p. 14) 4. gifted, talented (p. 24) 5. a, u, Muggie (p. 36) 6. principal, school psychologist (pp. 25–29) 7. computer (p. 28) 8. signature (p. 32) **B.** Answers will vary. Suggestions: because it is all wrinkled and stuck together, she could print and use the computer, books are not written in cursive, and because the more she gets pushed to write cursive the more contrary she becomes (pp. 8–12)

Quiz #2: A. 1. F (p. 37) 2. F (p. 41) 3. T (p. 47) 4. T (pp. 49–51) 5. T (p. 51) 6. F (p. 57) 7. T (p. 59) 8. F (p. 66) 9. F (p. 69) 10. F (p. 69) **B.** Answers will vary. Suggestions: She works all weekend by herself in her room, she studies every piece of cursive writing that she can find, she practices all the letters, she sees that many printed letters are like cursive letters, and she practices her signature (pp. 57–59).

Novel Test: A. 1. b (p. 18) 2. f (p. 28) 3. h (p. 31) 4. g (p. 53) 5. c (p. 41) 6. d (p. 14) 7. a (p. 25) 8. e (p. 11) **B.** 9. D (pp. 7–12) 10. C (throughout) 11. D (p. 32) 12. D (p. 36) 13. D (p. 47) 14. C (pp. 49–51) **C.** 15. Suggestion: She says books are not written in cursive (p. 12). 16. Suggestion: Maggie's parents and teacher become frustrated with her (p. 22). 17. Suggestions: Maggie writes fancy letters to Ms. Madden (p. 39). Maggie studies and practices cursive writing on her own over the weekend (p. 57). 18. Suggestion: Mrs. Leeper's method was successful. Maggie learned to read and write cursive. Answers will vary. Refer to the rubric on p. 26 of this guide.

Linking Novel Units® Student Packets to National and State Reading Assessments

During the past several years, an increasing number of students have faced some form of state-mandated competency testing in reading. Many states now administer state-developed assessments to measure the skills and knowledge emphasized in their particular reading curriculum. This Novel Units® guide includes open-ended comprehension questions that correlate with state-mandated reading assessments. The rubric below provides important information for evaluating responses to open-ended comprehension questions. Teachers may also use scoring rubrics provided for their own state's competency test.

Scoring Rubric for Open-Ended Items

3-Exemplary
Thorough, complete ideas/information
Clear organization throughout
Logical reasoning/conclusions
Thorough understanding of reading task
Accurate, complete response

2-Sufficient
Many relevant ideas/pieces of information
Clear organization throughout most of response
Minor problems in logical reasoning/conclusions
General understanding of reading task
Generally accurate and complete response

1-Partially Sufficient
Minimally relevant ideas/information
Obvious gaps in organization
Obvious problems in logical reasoning/conclusions
Minimal understanding of reading task
Inaccuracies/incomplete response

0-Insufficient
Irrelevant ideas/information
No coherent organization
Major problems in logical reasoning/conclusions
Little or no understanding of reading task
Generally inaccurate/incomplete response

Notes

Notes